W9-AWP-273

POLAR EXPLORATION
Courage and Controversy

BY DIANE BAILEY

POLAR EXPLORATION
Courage and Controversy

BY DIANE BAILEY

MASON CREST

Mason Crest

450 Parkway Drive, Suite D
Broomall, PA 19008
www.masoncrest.com

© 2018 by Mason Crest, an imprint of National Highlights, Inc.

Printed and bound in the United States of America.

First printing
1 3 5 7 9 8 6 4 2

Series ISBN: 978-1-4222-3863-9
ISBN: 978-1-4222-3870-7
ebook ISBN: 978-1-4222-7925-0

Library of Congress Cataloging-in-Publication Data on file with the publisher.

Developed and Produced by Shoreline Publishing Group.
Developmental Editor: James Buckley, Jr.
Design: Tom Carling, Carling Design Inc.
Production: Sandy Gordon
www.shorelinepublishing.com
Front cover: Courtesy Adrian Hayes; Library of Congress (inset).

QR Codes disclaimer:

CONTENTS

Key Icons to Look For

Words to Understand: These words with their easy-to-understand definitions will increase the reader's understanding of the text, while building vocabulary skills.

Sidebars: This boxed material within the main text allows readers to build knowledge, gain insights, explore possibilities, and broaden their perspectives by weaving together additional information to provide realistic and holistic perspectives.

Educational Videos: Readers can view videos by scanning our QR codes, providing them with additional educational content to supplement the text. Examples include news coverage, moments in history, speeches, iconic moments, and much more!

Text-Dependent Questions: These questions send the reader back to the text for more careful attention to the evidence presented here.

Research Projects: Readers are pointed toward areas of further inquiry connected to each chapter. Suggestions are provided for projects that encourage deeper research and analysis.

Series Glossary of Key Terms: This back-of-the-book glossary contains terminology used throughout this series. Words found here increase the reader's ability to read and comprehend higher-level books and articles in this field.

INTRODUCTION

What lies at the top of the world? That question has intrigued explorers for centuries. In the year 325 BCE, a Greek sailor named Pytheas sailed north. He told of finding a land of the "midnight sun," where the sun never set. He also described large sheets of ice and amazing colored lights that lit up the sky. Based on what we know now, historians think Pytheas was one of the first Europeans to reach the Arctic.

The southern tip of the world was another mystery. The ancient Greeks liked things to balance out. They figured if there was a large landmass in the north, then there must be one in the south as well. As it turned out, they were correct. Actually finding this "unknown southern land" took another 2,000 years, though. The northern polar regions were difficult enough to explore. The southern ones were nearly impossible.

Explorers ventured into the polar regions for many reasons. Some went seeking fame or to bring honor to their home country. Others were motivated by money. They hoped to cash in on the resources—from animal furs to precious metals—that these regions could offer. Still others went in the interest of science. They were eager to find out more about the geography of the earth and what might exist in different places.

It was a slow process. After Pytheas, it took another 1,000 years for Europeans to journey north again. It was several hundred years after that before exploration began in earnest. Exploring Antarctica took even longer. Rough seas turned back most adventurers until the 1700s. By the turn of the 1800s, though, polar exploration was in a golden age. Both poles were reached within a few years of each other in the early 1900s.

Today, exploration continues. There are new people, new equipment, and new goals. Still, the underlying reasons have not changed much. People are still interested in what the polar regions are like, and what they can teach us. And there are always a few who will go to the ends of the earth to find out.

Ships like these were the first to visit the Antarctic continent. Today, more advanced vessels make the journey, but this is actually a modern three-master.

The roadless stretches of snow and ice in the polar regions means that explorers need uncommon ways to get around, such as dogsledding.

Going to Extremes

1

Words to Understand

capsize   regarding a ship, to turn completely upside-down

dirigible   a type of airship that uses a lighter-than-air gas to float

hypothermia   a life-threatening condition of being too cold

satellite phone   a communications device that uses direct links between satellites

Planning to travel hundreds of miles into the icy unknown? You'd probably take sturdy, warm clothes, lots of nutritious food, and a good GPS system. You might pack a **satellite phone** just in case. Almost none of this was available to early polar explorers, but that did not stop them. They took the best supplies they had, some reliable companions, and, hopefully, a good dose of creativity. If they were smart and lucky, they might do okay. Still, even the most successful expeditions faced huge challenges.

Into the Arctic

The Arctic, the area surrounding the North Pole, was the first polar region to be explored. It is much closer to Europe, where most explorers came from. They already knew a little bit about it. Europeans had had some contact with native Arctic people for centuries.

An important reason to explore the Arctic was its position on the globe. Europe depended on trading with people in China, India, and Indonesia. Reaching those places from Western Europe was difficult. The journey over land meant dealing with robbers and rough terrain. The sea route, around the southern tip of Africa, was better, but still long and dangerous.

Europeans hoped there might be a northern route that would be faster and easier. In the 15th and 16th centuries, the world's geography was still being sketched out. At the time, Europeans believed that China and India were not as far away as they really are. The Arctic Ocean is perched at the top of the globe. They thought going across it could be the perfect shortcut. Looking for this "northwest passage" became the goal of many explorers. In addition, explorers hoped to cash in on the resources of the Arctic. Seal furs, ivory walrus tusks, and whale oil were valuable items in European markets.

The idea of finding a passage was simple in concept. In practice it was extremely difficult. Expedition after expedition set out. The lucky ones returned only to report their failure. The unlucky ones were never heard from again. Many explorers died

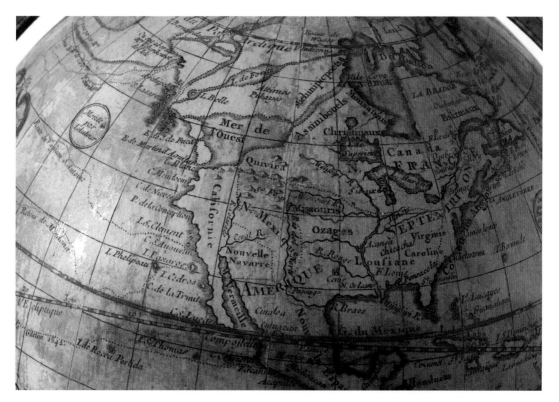

The lands to the north of North America were mostly unknown for millennia. Globes such as this one often showed more water and less land than was actually there.

looking for a northwest passage, but the idea itself stayed very much alive. A northwest passage was finally found—but it took about 400 years! By that time there were new goals for exploring the Arctic, however. The biggest was getting to the North Pole.

The Unknown Southern Land

For most explorers, the Arctic offered fame and fortune. Did the Antarctic have the same prizes? No one knew. In fact, until the late 1700s, no one knew for sure that Antarctica even existed!

There were clues that it did. Voyages in the 1500s and 1600s pushed farther and farther south, closer to *terra australis incognita*, the "unknown southern land." A lot of that travel was not by choice. Terrible storms blew ships off course, into the island chains surrounding Antarctica. Sailors came back with stories about mountains made of snow, and large sheets of ice in the ocean. Still, no one had seen the Antarctic continent as of the late 1700s. And what had been seen didn't seem very promising.

Sailors venturing in the far southern oceans in wooden sailing ships braved high winds and ice floes, but they did get to meet penguins.

A couple of things kept Antarctic exploration going. One was seals. Sailors had found huge seal populations in the south, and sealing was a big industry at the time. That was enough reason for many to keep going back. Another incentive was scientific curiosity. What did Antarctica look like? Did anyone live there? If nothing else, Antarctica had a landmark: the South Pole. That was enough to make it a destination.

Against the Odds

For many polar explorers, the goal was getting there before anyone else. But before that could happen, they had to figure out where "there" was. Well into the 1800s, many maps of the polar regions were incomplete and inaccurate. Maps were drawn based on a handful of past reports, and a whole lot of guessing. Sometimes they were just completely made up. Lots of times mapmakers did not know what a certain area was like — but they were pretty sure it was bad. They labeled such regions with pictures

Tall Tales

In 1588, the Spanish sailor Laurent Ferrer Maldonado came home with a great story. He'd breezed through the Arctic Ocean through what he called the "Strait of Anian." There, he'd seen Russian ships stocked with products from China. According to Maldonado, the Northwest Passage was not only there, but also was easy to get through. Maldonado's tale had just one problem: He'd probably made it up. Why? One theory is that he wanted money. Polar expeditions were expensive. The money for them came from governments, such as Spain. That would help Maldonado's case.

Explorers to the Antarctic also had some tall tales to tell. In the late 1770s, a French explorer named Yves-Joseph de Kergulen-Trmarec traveled to the Antarctic. He hoped to find a place with mild weather and a friendly landscape. Guess what? He returned with just such a story. According to him, "New South France" was ready and waiting. Of course, he was wrong, but the idea of such a place was enough for the French government. They sent him back to look some more. The next time, he had to admit his mistake.

of sea monsters, shipwrecks, and warnings like, "Here are lions."

There are no lions at either pole, but without reliable information, it was not unusual for explorers to get lost. As if that wasn't bad enough, neither the Arctic nor Antarctica has good weather for traveling. Both are cold, and Antarctica is brutal in the winter. Temperatures can sink below −100° F (−73° C). Storms in the ocean make huge waves that can **capsize** even the most seaworthy vessels.

And then there's the ice. Until the 19th century, ships were built of wood. Unfortunately, wood is no match for ice. Even when powered by engines later in the century, the ships could not push through ice that was several feet thick. Many unlucky sailors became encased in the ice as winter set in. They could be frozen into place for months at a time. Even the rough seas of open water were welcome compared to being trapped, with shrinking supplies of food and fuel to stay warm. Worse, the freezing ice would squeeze a ship from all sides. Sometimes the ships cracked under the pressure. Many sailors were forced to abandon their vessels. They piled into lifeboats or just onto the ice itself, in desperate attempts to make it to safety.

Travel was difficult on the ice itself, too. Explorers had to be careful to avoid crevasses, which are deep gaps in the ice that are easy to fall into. They also had to be careful not to travel on ice that was too thin to support them, or that would float away from where they wanted to go. Most explorers walked or skied, using teams of dogs trained to pull sledges over the ice. Some-

Siberian huskies are trained to work in packs to pull sleds loaded with people and gear over snow and ice. Some take part in races as well.

times they used ponies. The animals could carry supplies, and they could be used as food later in the journey. One explorer even tried using reindeer to pull his sledges. It didn't work, though. The reindeer ran away!

Early explorers also had very little knowledge about how to survive in extreme cold. They brought the warmest clothing they had, usually made of wool. Wool is fine for a chilly European winter, but it's not so good in frigid temperatures. Worse, it loses its ability to insulate when it gets wet. **Hypothermia** and frostbite were common for early explorers.

Food was another problem. Polar explorers needed food that was high in protein and calories, and that would not spoil. A common type of food to take was pemmican, which is dried meat and animal fat. That was a good start, but it did not have enough calories for men who were hauling heavy sleds over the ice in the punishing cold. (Plus, they got bored eating it all the time.)

Better Methods

Massive icebreakers such as this Russian craft (that's why the Cyrillic "R" is backward) can now crash through thick ice to create new passageways through polar waters.

Advances in technology helped polar exploration tremendously by the late 19th century. The invention of the gasoline motor in the 1800s opened up a new world of possibilities. Explorers could put motors on their sledges. By the 1950s, they had snowmobiles.

Wooden ships gave way to much sturdier ones made from aluminum and steel. In the 1930s, icebreaker ships that ran on diesel fuel were being built to plow through the thick ice of the poles. They had huge, heavy prows (fronts) that broke through thick ice. By the 1950s, nuclear technology was also used for those ships. Airplanes were another possibility.

Compared to a century ago, polar exploration is easy now. Tourists can sail to Antarctica on a cruise ship, or visit the North Pole on board a nuclear icebreaker. (You don't have to be in good shape, but you'd better have some money—the trips cost a lot!) Adventurous explorers are always looking for new ways to travel. Some have even explored

The View From Above

Since traveling on the ground was so difficult, why not rise above it? That's what some early explorers decided to do. In 1897, Swedish explorer S.A. Andrée decided to fly to the North Pole in a hydrogen balloon. Unfortunately, he did not have a good way to steer. He crashed after only two days. A better form of air travel was coming, though. In 1903, the airplane was invented. Richard Byrd, an American pilot, made headlines when he reportedly flew an airplane over the North Pole in 1926. (However, his record of the trip shows he might not quite have reached there.) Not far behind him was Roald Amundsen. Just three days after Byrd claimed to fly over the North Pole, Amundsen floated over it in a **dirigible**. Byrd would still earn a place in the history books. In 1929, he flew over the South Pole. Today, flights regularly go to Antarctica, but only in the summer. Only one type of plane in the world—the Twin Otter—can fly in the extreme cold of an Antarctic winter. It is only used for emergencies.

The Amundsen-Scott Research Station (named for two famous explorers we'll meet soon) is run by the United States not far from the South Pole.

the polar regions on bicycles!

Scientists stationed at the poles stay warm and comfortable with electricity and hot water. They can eat fresh food flown in by airplanes (except during the Antarctic winter). They dress in layers, with fleece hats, down jackets, and clothes made with other synthetic materials that keep them warm. They can communicate with phones and by email, and do their work with computers.

Early explorers could not have imagined such luxuries.

Many things were stacked against them, and every step was a new battle. Still, they set out optimistically. When they returned, they brought new stories—and new questions—to inspire the next party.

 # Text-Dependent Questions

1. What was a main reason Europeans first began to explore the Arctic?

2. How did ice make traveling difficult for ships?

3. What is pemmican?

 # Research Project

Find pictures of maps that were made several centuries ago, before people knew a lot about the polar regions. Compare them to modern maps. What things did mapmakers get right? What were way off?

South Pole station tour

American explorer Robert Peary won the "race" to the North Pole, reaching the geographic top of the world after a long walk in 1909.

To the Top

2

Words to Understand

axis an imaginary line that goes through the center of an object

Inuit people native to the Arctic

meteorology the study of weather

mutiny a strong, often violent, rebellion against authority

Reaching the North Pole was a distant dream before the 19th century. Early explorers did not have enough knowledge, or the right equipment, to successfully make the journey. That was okay. Sure, planting a flag at the top of the Arctic was something to be proud of. Finding a way *through* the Arctic, though, would be much more useful.

This painting shows English explorer Henry Hudson (white beard) with his son after they were cast adrift by a mutinous crew in 1611.

First Steps

By the 16th century, countries in Europe were heavily involved in trading. One of the biggest markets was in the East Indies, including China and India. Making the trip over land was difficult and dangerous, so explorers began looking for a water route across the Arctic Ocean. The search for a "northwest passage" occupied explorers for centuries.

One of the first to head out was the Italian sailor John Cabot, in 1497. He did not find a passage, but he did make it to Canada (although he thought it was Asia). Cabot's son Sebastian tried again in 1508, but with no better results than his father. The English got into the game in 1576, when Martin Frobisher went looking. He also made it to Canada, but still no passage. Next up was the Englishman John Davis in 1585 and the Dutch sailor William Barents a decade after that. Again, no luck.

In 1607, the English explorer Henry Hudson decided to take a turn—but in the other direction. Most explorers before him had looked for a northwest passage across the Arctic. Hudson decided to go east instead. After he failed on two attempts, he went back to the northwest idea. Hudson's third voyage (to the west) was also unsuccessful, but he was not discouraged. In 1610, he set out on his fourth trip. Unfortunately, his ship, the *Discovery*, got stuck in the ice in what is now Hudson Bay, Canada. Winter stayed late in the year 1611, and the crew of the *Discovery* became desperate. As food ran low, some of them held a **mutiny**. They forced Hudson, his teenage son, and some other crew members to get into a lifeboat. Then they lowered it into the water and cut it loose from the main ship. Hudson, his son, and the other men in their boat were never seen again. (The crew of the main ship did get back to England.)

Over the next couple of centuries, there were more voyages into the Arctic. No one found a passage—northwest or north-east—and no one got to the North Pole. But those voyages were not failures. Each explorer mapped a little bit more of the Arctic. They found new islands and bays. They got a better picture of the coastline. Bit by bit, they were drawing a clearer picture of the Arctic.

Looking for Franklin

One explorer was British ship captain John Franklin. He went on several polar journeys in the early 1800s. One that he led from 1819–1822 had terrible consequences. The weather was worse than usual, the food ran out, and more than half of the people in the party died from starvation or disease. Franklin himself survived, though. He got the nickname of "the man who ate his boots." (That's what you do when you're starving.)

Despite that disaster, the British government still thought Franklin was a good explorer. They sent him out again in 1845 to look for the northwest passage. This time, things went even worse than they had 20 years earlier. Two years went by, and no one had gotten any word from the expedition. Franklin's wife convinced the government to send out a search party. When they didn't find anything, another search party went out. And another. And another. No one found Franklin's ships (they re-mained missing until 2014), but the searchers pieced together what had happened. They talked to the local **Inuit** population

There were no photographers on the ill-fated Franklin expedition to the Arctic, but an artist made this drawing based on reports.

in Canada, which reported seeing a party of white men who had starved. Then they found a few abandoned supplies, some graves, and some letters and notes from people on the expedition. The searches for Franklin took the lives of more men than the original expedition. But the voyages did help map much of the Canadian polar region.

The innovative design of the Fram, *the ship of Norwegian explorer Fridtjof Nansen, showed future polar travelers new ways to tackle the thick ice.*

New Ideas

A northwest passage was finally discovered in 1851. (It took another 50 years for the Norwegian explorer Roald Amundsen to actually sail through it, however.) Then, in 1879, a north*east* passage was found. By that time, however, the focus of Arctic exploration was turning to science. An Austrian explorer, Carl Weyprecht, wanted scientists from all over the world to cooperate in studying the poles. They could collect data on everything from geology to **meteorology**. He proposed the idea of an International Polar Year dedicated to this idea. The IPY actually lasted three years. It began in 1881 and ended in 1884. Scientists from 11 different countries set up research stations in the Arctic.

Through their travels and experiences, explorers had become more knowledgeable about the best ways to travel in the Arctic. At first, Europeans and had used large ships, brought their own food, and tried to adapt their own ways of survival to the Arctic. But by the late 19th century, the most successful expeditions used smaller ships that carried explorers who adopted the survival techniques used by people native to the Arctic. They ate fresh meat to fight off scurvy, a disease caused by not getting enough Vitamin C. They found that clothing made from animal furs was much better than wool or cloth.

A persistent problem was the ice. Ships could be pushed off course by the drifting ice, or crushed when it froze them in. In 1878, the United States launched an expedition on the *Jeanette*, which got trapped in ice and then sank in 1881. A few years later, wreckage from the *Jeanette* washed up on the coast of Greenland. It was almost 3,000 miles (4,828 km) from where the ship had sunk!

That information was very interesting to the Norwegian explorer Fridtjof Nansen. From the location of the wreckage, he learned how the currents flowed in the Arctic Ocean. It gave him an idea. Most explorers looked for ways to avoid getting stuck in the drifting ice. Nansen thought maybe that's exactly what he

Moving Target

Early explorers looking for the North Pole had a decision to make: which North Pole to shoot for? There is actually more than one! The magnetic North Pole is where the Earth's magnetic field points straight downward. (A compass needle would actually "dip" and point down, so this is also called a "dip pole.") The other is the geographic North Pole. Imagine the planet's **axis**, an imaginary vertical rod that runs straight through the middle of the globe. The place where that rod comes out the top is the geographic North Pole. This location does not stay in one place however. Geographers have found that as the planet spins, it wobbles a little bit. It moves about 30 feet (9.1 m) over 7 years. Where the North Pole is at any given time is called the "instantaneous pole."

should do. He reasoned that if the ice did not destroy a ship, it could carry it along instead.

Nansen built a ship called the *Fram*. It had a specially designed, rounded hull that looked like an egg. When the ice froze, it would not crush the ship. Instead, the movement would just push the ship up. The ship would sit on top and drift along with the ice. Then, Nansen would just wait for it to cross over the North Pole. Many people thought Nansen's idea was crazy, but he went ahead with his plan. The ship worked just the way Nansen thought it would. Unfortunately, it did not get close enough to the pole. Nansen had shown, however, that traveling with the ice was more effective than trying to fight against it. Later explorers would take advantage of his clever idea.

The Push to the Pole

At the turn of the century, much of the world caught "polar fever." The Arctic had been mapped enough so that sailors could get around reliably. They knew more about how the ice behaved, and their ships were stronger. Radios let them communicate with the outside world. Getting to the North Pole wasn't just a dream anymore—it was in reach.

British and European explorers had led the way in polar exploration for centuries. By the early 1900s, two Americans, Frederick Cook and Robert Peary, had joined the race. Peary had always been obsessed with reaching the North Pole. After a few

Just south of the Arctic Circle in Alaska stands the tallest peak in North America. Once known as Mt. McKinley, the peak has been reverted to its native name of Denali.

adventures of his own, Cook decided he wanted that prize, too. Cook needed to raise money for an expedition to the North Pole. He sponsored a trip to climb Alaska's Mount McKinley (now called Denali). Then he wrote a book about reaching the summit. That helped get him recognized as a competent explorer and obtain the funding he needed.

Cook set off in 1907 and returned the next year. He claimed he reached the North Pole on April 21, 1908. Meanwhile, before Cook's news became public, Peary had started his own journey to the pole. He said he got there on April 6, 1909. When he announced that, however, he found out that Cook had claimed to have reached there almost an entire year earlier.

What made it all so complicated is that no one knew for sure if either man had really reached the pole. Some of Cook's descriptions sounded like the North

Frederick Cook claimed to have reached the North Pole a year earlier than Robert Peary, but his status as the "first" is now very much a question mark.

Pole, but others did not. Some of his measurements were not accurate. Peary's story also had some holes in it. Based on the dates he recorded, he would have had to travel 30 miles (48 km) a day. That was a staggering amount over the rough Arctic landscape. Neither man had a witness to support his claims. Also, the North Pole is not on land—it's on ice that's on top of water. Even though Peary planted a flag on the ice above the North Pole, it would have drifted away. Later explorers would not be able to find the flag and back up his claim.

An investigation finally handed the prize to Peary. (It did not help that Cook's account of reaching the summit of Mount McKinley turned out to be false.) For the next several decades, Peary held the title of "first." Then, in 1988, historians decided to look at Peary's account again. With better technology to test Peary's evidence, they decided Peary actually had not reached the pole. Whether either man really did is still up for debate. Without clear evidence to support either one, the official title had to go to someone else. But who?

Again, the question is a little sticky. There are actually several ways to reach the Pole, by water, land, and air. In 1926, Richard Byrd said he flew over the North Pole in a small plane. (Like many other claims, this one is in dispute.) Just a few days later, Roald Amundsen floated above it in a dirigible. The U.S. submarine *Nautilus* passed under it in 1958. But if the real prize is reaching the

North Pole controversy

There is no dispute that Wally Herbert (left) reached the North Pole in 1969. He got there the old-fashioned way—by dogsled.

North Pole by land, then perhaps the winner is Ralph Plaisted. He crossed the ice in a snowmobile and reached the Pole in 1968. Also worth remembering is the British explorer Wally Herbert. In 1969, he became the first to get there the old-fashioned way, by dogsled, without anyone contesting his claim.

Whoever was first, once the Pole was reached, exploration of the Arctic could turn more firmly toward science and away from racing!

Text-Dependent Questions

1. What nickname did British captain John Franklin get?

2. Why did Fridtjof Nansen's ship the *Fram* do better sailing in ice?

3. Who made the first claim for reaching the North Pole?

 # Research Project

Look up and read the accounts given by Robert Peary and Frederick Cook about reaching the North Pole. What do you think about their reports? Do you believe either one of them—or both—actually made it?

The Norwegian explorer Roald Amundsen gained worldwide fame for leading the expedition that was the first to reach the South Pole.

Going South

③

Words to Understand

commodity   a basic material that is bought and sold

convergence   the act of two or more things coming together

hospitable   friendly, welcoming, safe

morale   the overall mood and attitude of a person or group

pelts   furred animal skins

treacherous   extremely difficult or dangerous

Five and a half million square miles (14,250,000 sq km) of ice. That's what was waiting for sailors who managed to get through the **treacherous** Southern Ocean to Antarctica. The continent is not a very **hospitable** place for humans, but early explorers had no way of knowing that. Writings by the ancient Greeks and Romans told of a land that was a tropical paradise where lots of friendly folks lived. Europeans had no reason to doubt that image. Why not pay a visit?

An Elusive Continent

Throughout the 1500s and 1600s, plenty of sailors went looking for the "unknown southern land." Bit by bit, they got farther south, but actually reaching the continent was extremely difficult. One problem was the Antarctic **Convergence**. That is where strong, cold currents flowing north from Antarctica meet warmer ones heading south. When they do, it often causes severe storms. Many sailors, in their wooden sailing ships, had to turn back from the rough waters.

Yet explorers were convinced something was there, if they could just get to it. In 1767, the Scottish geographer Alexander Dalrymple published a report that supported the idea of a southern land. The British government thought he was on to something. They sent the British navy captain James Cook to investigate. From 1772 to 1775, Cook circled the whole Antarctic continent. The funny part is, he never actually saw it! He got within about 80 miles of the shore, but the ice would not let him go closer. Cook's voyage did convince him of one thing: The southern polar regions were uninhabitable and worthless.

Except, that is, for the seals and whales.

Cook had seen plenty of those animals. They lived around the continent of Antarctica and also slightly farther north, near the Falkland Islands and Sandwich Islands. Sealing and whaling were big business at the time. Seal **pelts**, whale oil, and whale bones were valuable **commodities**. Hunters were more than willing to brave the dangers of the Antarctic if it meant money—and it did.

This is a modern recreation of the Endeavour, *the famous ship led by Captain James Cook on its world-spanning journey, which included circumnavigation of Antarctica.*

Over the next 50 years, thousands of hunters swarmed into the region. When they wiped out the animal population in one area, they moved on to another. In fact, it was the search for seals that probably led to the first person walking on the Antarctic continent. Although there's no absolute proof, records suggest that in 1821, an American sealing captain named John Davis landed his ship on the Antarctic mainland. The men got off and walked around for a little while. They did not find any seals, though, so they left after less than an hour.

From Seals to Science

Even though their primary focus was hunting, some sealers and whalers also had an interest in science. Many discovered and named new islands and helped map the coastline. They found fossils of ancient animals. One explorer and scientist was James Weddell, who sailed to the Antarctic a couple of years after John Davis. Weddell was a sealer, but he was also one of the world's first environmentalists. He saw how sealers before him had been reckless in their hunting habits, destroying whole populations. Weddell pointed out that if the animals had been hunted more responsibly, the populations would have survived.

By the 1830s, the seal populations were mostly wiped out. Sealers were no longer interested in the area, but governments were. The United States, Britain, and France all sent expeditions. Everyone wanted to discover new land they could claim for their countries. They also hoped to find the South Pole.

James Clark Ross sailed from England in 1839 to look for the pole. By January 1841 he had traveled farther south than anyone else before him. In fact, he had gone as far as it was possible to go by ship. The American explorer Charles Wilkes traveled to the continent at about the same time as Ross. Both of them found more islands and mapped more of the Antarctic coastline. But the South Pole itself was still out of their grasp. It lay inland, over miles of ice. Getting there would involve even more difficult travel.

Antarctic exploration became less popular after that. For about 50 years, the focus was on the North Pole, not the south. Then, in 1893, a whaling ship set off from Norway to Antarctica. As a hunting expedition, the trip was a failure. The men even got into a scuffle with the local penguin population! However, crew

Today's polar visitors can arrive on high-tech metal ships that come with advanced navigation gear, living quarters, and ice-breaking capability.

members did make an important discovery when they landed in Antarctica in 1895. They found lichen, a combination of fungus and algae that looks like moss. This was the first evidence that anything could grow on the Antarctic continent. Now, countries around the world got interested again in exploring the continent. The "heroic age" of Antarctic exploration was starting.

Roald Amundsen used dog sleds for part of his journey to the North Pole. For the final push to the Pole, he and his men walked and used skis.

The Heroic Age

The pace of Antarctic exploration was moving faster than ever before. Now that sailors knew how to reach the continent, they began to push inland. On skis and sleds, the race to reach the South Pole began.

One seasoned explorer was Roald Amundsen. He had done a lot of exploring in the Arctic. In 1906 he became the first person to take a ship all the way through the northwest passage. By 1909, he hoped to be the first person to reach the North Pole, but he was too late. Frederick Cook and Robert Peary were already wrestling for that title. Amundsen decided on a new goal—he even already a ship ready to go. In fact, it was the *Fram*, the ship specially built by his countryman Fridtjof Nansen to cross the Arctic. Instead of sailing to the Arctic, however, Amundsen turned south. His crew was in for a surprise. He didn't even tell them that he'd changed plans until they were well on their way!

Staying Alive

Eat healthy. Get some sun. Keep your spirits up. All good advice, but it can be pretty difficult to follow in the depths of a polar winter. Frederick Cook (who later claimed to reach the North Pole) was a doctor on an 1897 expedition to Antarctica. When the ship, the *Belgica*, got stuck in the ice, the party had to spend the whole winter on the icy continent. It was the first time anyone had had to do that, and it was a terrible experience. The members of the crew showed signs of scurvy. Fresh meat provides Vitamin C to fight scurvy, but the ship's captain thought eating raw seals and penguins was gross. He wouldn't let his men eat it. Finally, Cook took over. He convinced the captain to let the crew eat fresh meat to help the scurvy. He also knew it was important to keep the men's **morale** positive. He had the crew play card games—betting pretend money—to entertain themselves. He also made sure the sailors spent time every day in front of an open fire. This was a kind of "light therapy." It helped them fight depression from not getting any sunlight through the dark winter.

Amundsen had some competition in his quest for the South Pole. A British naval officer named Robert Falcon Scott also wanted to travel there. The two men had different goals. Amundsen was just concerned with just getting to the pole first. Scott, however, was interested in science. He had already done many experiments in the polar regions. He wanted to use his journey to the South Pole to do more. As a result, the two men took very different approaches in their travel to the pole.

Using dogs to pull the sleds, Amundsen's men would also use skis. Scott used a combination of dogs, ponies, and motorized sleds. Scott's team was also larger. Those things proved to be mistakes. The sleds broke down and there was no one to fix them. Many of the ponies died. Scott moved more slowly, and his men had to work harder. They used up their supplies faster.

Amundsen set up his base camp about 60 miles (97 km) closer to the pole than Scott, which would save him some time when the final trek began. Scott, on the other hand, chose a site that was good for exploring the geology. After landing and spending the winter on the mainland, both men set out within two weeks of each other in late 1911 to cross the ice and reach the pole. (Amundsen left first.)

Many stories about traveling on the Antarctic continent are filled with details about extreme cold, lack of food, and terrible dangers. Amundsen's journey was not one of them. The trip went fairly easily. He reached the pole on December 14, 1911. He put up a Norwegian flag and left a note for Scott, whom he assumed was close behind.

Members of the ill-fated Scott expedition took this photo when they reached the Pole, but only the picture made it back; the men died on the return trip. Scott is back row center.

Scott was on his way, but his party did not reach the pole for almost another month. When they found Amundsen had already been there, they were terribly disappointed. It was only going to get worse. The choices Scott had made in planning his trip caught up with him. When the men started their return trip, they were already tired, hungry, and low on supplies. When storms delayed them even more, they knew they were finished. They huddled up in a tent, wrote notes to their families, and died.

Shackleton's Journey

One name always comes up when talking about Antarctic explorers: Ernest Shackleton. Shackleton took many polar journeys and tried to reach the South Pole in 1908. He had to turn back, and was disappointed when Amundsen beat him there a few years later. But there was still another prize to win. No one had yet crossed the entire Antarctic continent, coast to coast. Shackleton decided to try in 1914.

The voyage went wrong almost from the start. Shackleton's ship, *Endurance*, got trapped in ice less than 100 miles from where the party needed to be. For nine months, the crew was stranded on board. Then, in November, the strength of the ice overpowered the ship. It cracked the hull, and the *Endurance* sank. Shackleton and his men bailed out onto the ice with some supplies and lifeboats. It still took another five months before they could continue to travel. During that time, they lived on the ice, eating seals and then even their sled dogs. Finally, they were able to try to reach Elephant Island, about 100 miles (161 km) away. Stuffed into the small lifeboats, and bailing constantly against the storms, the men made it there a week later.

The Shackleton story

Next was an even bigger challenge. To get help, they needed to reach a whaling camp on South Georgia Island. It was 800 miles (1,287 km) north, across one of the roughest seas in the world. Six men, including Shackleton, set off in one of the lifeboats, the *James Caird*. It was an incredibly dangerous voyage. Twenty-foot (6-m) waves hammered the boat. The men fought to keep their balance and stay on board. Somehow they made it.

The amazing Ernest Shackleton adventure has remained in the public eye in part because numerous glass-plate photos survived as well, such as this of the ship in ice.

This photo includes the men that Shackleton left behind on Elephant Island while he and a small crew left on a perilous 800-mile journey to get help. All survived.

It is considered one of the most courageous and amazing small-boat journeys ever made.

Even after that, the exhausted crew members had to hike for more than 20 miles (32 km) to reach the camp, crossing an uncharted glacier with almost no equipment. They hammered nails point-out through their shoes to get a grip on the ice. They also had to stay awake the entire time—sleeping would mean death.

Shackleton knew he could not give up. The rest of his men were still stuck back on Elephant Island, waiting for him. Shackleton was a remarkable leader, keeping the spirits of his men up and leading them through each step of a perilous journey. Four months later, they returned to get their companions. The men who had stayed behind were close to starving, living on snails. Shackleton had arrived just in time. All 28 men who sailed with the *Endurance* lived to tell their story.

 # Text-Dependent Questions:

1. What is the Antarctic Convergence?

2. What did the doctor Frederick Cook do to help the members of his crew fight scurvy?

3. What is one reason Robert Scott's expedition to the South Pole had trouble?

 # Research Project

The British geologist Sir Raymond Priestley once said, "For scientific leadership, give me Scott; for swift and efficient travel, Amundsen; but when you are in a hopeless situation, [give me] Shackleton." Each of those Antarctic explorers had a different style. Choose one and research his early efforts as an explorer. What events influenced him later in life?

British soldier Adrian Hayes was a busy guy in 2007. He became the first person to walk to both the North and South Poles in the same year.

Modern Exploration

Words to Understand

desalination   the process of removing salt from water

ecosystem   a group of plants, animals, and other environmental features that interact with each other

floe   an ice sheet floating in the water

replica   an exact copy of another object

treaty   a formal agreement

turbine   a machine that creates electricity by rotating; often powered by wind or water

By the early 1900s, both of the poles had been conquered, but that did not mean that polar exploration was finished. Instead, it just took a different direction. The next generation of polar explorers found new ways to travel and new things to study.

Setting up Shop

After the first International Polar Year in 1881, another was held 50 years later, from 1932–33. For it, even more nations joined in to do scientific experiments at the poles. In 1937, Russian scientists established the first North Pole research station, called NP–1. Because the North Pole is in the middle of the sea, however, that station was an actually a large ice **floe** in the water. The scientists on the NP–1 mission used the ice itself as their "ship." They traveled wherever the ice took them. The men had tents, food, a radio, a dog, equipment to take measurements from the ocean, and a chess game. They stayed on the floe for nine months before it started to break up. They radioed for help, and an icebreaker ship came to rescue them.

Today, people still go out on "drifting" stations in the Arctic to do research. They collect data about the ocean depth and temperature, chemicals in the water, the thickness of the ice, the flow of the currents, the atmosphere, and marine biology. However, a lot of research in the Arctic is now done remotely. Floating buoys can be put on the ice to collect information that is then picked up by satellites. Some of the buoys have long ropes attached to them. They can drop down 2,000 feet (610 m) into the water. A small tube travels down the rope and takes measurements far beneath the surface. There are also robot submarines and unmanned vehicles that can stay underwater for months as they get data.

Research in Antarctica has different challenges. The continent is colder, and harder to get in and out of. On the other hand, it's

The McMurdo Research Station in Antarctica is almost a small town, with fuel tanks, living quarters, recreation, roads, and more.

on land, so at least it doesn't move around. A permanent research station was set up on Antarctica in 1903. Now there are several run by various countries.

One is McMurdo Station, operated by the United States. Life at McMurdo shows that living in the polar regions is not nearly as hard as it once was. At McMurdo, scientists live in heated buildings, with computers and connections to the Internet. They

Bundled up against the cold, the staff at the American-run McMurdo-Scott Research Station gathers (quickly!) for a team photo.

get electricity from wind **turbines** and oil-powered generators. **Desalination** machines convert seawater into freshwater for drinking. Professional chefs make their meals. When they are not working, they watch movies, play pool, listen to live bands, have art shows, and even run marathons!

There are also many smaller research stations scattered across the country, but they are not as fancy. At the South Pole Station, workers have to chop ice and melt it for water. Showers have to be really short—only two minutes twice a week. However, there's a library and even a store for basic necessities. It has a sign in front that says, "Store in a cold, dry place."

Looking Closer

For the last century, the main adventure at both poles has been science. The poles are ideal places to study all different kinds of science. Workers do research into geology, biology, meteorology, climatology, and astronomy.

Some amazing scientific discoveries have been made through polar study. In 1982, a scientist named Joseph Farman was collecting data about the atmosphere in Antarctica. He noticed that there was a big "hole" in the ozone layer. Ozone is a gas in the air that helps protect the earth from harmful radiation from the sun. The hole was huge—the size of the United States. Scientists thought that chlorofluorocarbons (CFCs), chemicals that were often used in spray cans, like hair spray or air freshener, were probably causing the problem. Countries around the world took action and stopped using so many CFCs. Now, 35 years later, the hole in the ozone is much smaller. A 2016 treaty banned a CFC replacement called HFC that was also proving dangerous.

Animal research is another hot topic. From polar bears in the north to whales and penguins in the south, biologists can study how certain animals can live in extreme cold.

HFC agreement reached

Not every polar research topic is Earth-bound. Here, a scientist poses with a meteorite, one of thousands that strike the poles each year.

They also research how animals are responding to environmental threats such as global warming. In recent years, scientists have found viruses in the Arctic. For tens of thousands of years, the viruses were buried a hundred feet under the ice. Now the ice is melting and the viruses are thawing out. Even after all this time, the viruses are still able to infect organisms. The good news is that the viruses are a little behind the times. They evolved to infect single-celled creatures, so they aren't a threat to modern humans or animals.

Antarctica is a particularly good place to study meteorites. These dark pieces of rock from outer space are easy to spot in the white snow, and they don't erode very fast in the cold, dry air. Scientists have also noticed there are a lot of similarities between Antarctica and the planet Mars. Studying the cold continent may help them understand more about the climate of Mars.

Even the scientists doing research are being studied. Workers at the poles spend a lot of time in the dark, just like astronauts. Researchers from NASA are investigating how the lack of sunlight affects the human body, so they can better prepare astronauts for long periods in the darkness of space.

Staking a Claim

Early polar explorers often claimed the land for their home countries. In many cases, though, they never followed up on those claims. That may be changing,

It's Hot Out There

Scientists have known about global warming for decades. The Earth's overall temperature is heating up faster than ever, which is causing changes in ecosystems everywhere. It seems a little crazy, but the coldest places on Earth are among the best places to study global warming. That's because scientists can actually see what's happening. Satellite photos show how much ice in the polar regions today has shrunk compared to several years ago.

Unfortunately, the ice is melting away very fast. The poles are warming up faster than anywhere else in the world. The white surface of ice reflects heat back into the atmosphere. When there is less ice, more heat is absorbed into the water and that melts more ice. Also, warm water from other parts of the world flows in on ocean currents and melts the ice from below. Scientists have also found ways to calculate the age of ice in the polar regions. Some of it is hundreds of years old. However, they now know that a lot of the ice is much "younger," only formed in the last few years. The base of older ice is getting smaller.

especially in the Arctic. The Arctic has lots of natural resources, including coal, iron, gold, and silver, and, most importantly, huge reserves of oil and natural gas.

In the past, it was not always worth it to get those resources. They were buried under the ice, and digging them out was difficult and expensive. Global warming has changed things. There is less ice, and it is easier to drill, as well as easier to go by ship through the Arctic waters because there is not as much as ice blocking the way. Some countries, including the United States and Russia, are already drilling for oil in the Arctic. Many scientists and environmentalists think this is a bad idea, and that more

The potential for oil and gas drilling in the Arctic has to be balanced against the huge danger of environmental damage to this sensitive area.

drilling is a worse idea. That would mean more people, more buildings, more roads, and more traffic. All of that could ruin the region's fragile **ecosystems**.

The situation in Antarctica is somewhat different. The continent belongs to no one—or everyone, depending on how you look at it. In 1961, an international **treaty** went into effect to protect the continent. It said countries could send teams there for scientific research, but that it could only be used for peaceful purposes. In 1998 another agreement went into effect. It protected the environment of Antarctica by saying that mining resources was not allowed. So far, that arrangement is working out. One reason is that the region does not have easy-to-reach resources and it would be risky and expensive to get to them. But in 30 years things could be different as better technology and melting ice may make it easier to find and harvest resources. When the agreement expires in 2048, everything could go up for grabs.

Following in Their Footsteps

Science and commerce are the main focus of polar exploration today. But there are always people who simply want adventure. There is always some new place to go and some new way to get there.

Early explorers set out in teams. Now, many people have made solo journeys. In 1994, Borge Ousland, a Norwegian explorer, made the first unsupported solo trip to the North Pole, meaning he did not get any help along the way. A few years later, he crossed Antarctica alone and unsupported.

Tim Jarvis and his crew matched the feat of Shackleton, recreating the small-boat journey that the British adventurer made more than a century earlier.

In 2007, Adrian Hayes, a former British soldier, set a world record by walking to both the South and North Poles in the same year (along with climbing to the top of Mt. Everest!).

Some expeditions recreate the historic ones of the early 20th century. British explorer Tom Avery was curious whether Robert Peary really could have reached the North Pole. In 2009, 100 years after Peary, Avery put together a team to try it. His team used the same equipment, and followed the same 800-mile (1,287 km) route Peary had. Afterward, Avery said he believed Peary could have done it.

In 2013, almost 100 years after Ernest Shackleton's famous Antarctic journey, the British-Australian explorer Tim Jarvis decided to do it again—exactly the same way. Jarvis ordered a **replica** of the boat that Shackleton used back in 1914. His clothing and other supplies also were the same kind used in that time.

That same year, Britons Ben Saunders and Tarka L'Herpiniere decided to retrace Robert Scott's journey to the South Pole. They used modern equipment that was lighter and sturdier, and they packed a lot more food. On the flip side, they did not have any dogs or ponies to help them, as Scott did, and they pulled all their own supplies on sleds. The 1,800-mile (2,897-km) trip took more than three months.

Teenagers are getting in on the action, too. A group of four 13-year-olds from Norway walked to the North Pole in 2015. They traveled 69 miles (111 km) in six days—four days faster than they had planned!

Journeys to the North Pole may be coming to an end, though. Most of them start from northern points of the US, Canada, Russia, or Greenland. From

Women of the Polar Regions

Josephine Peary went to the Arctic with her husband, Robert, in the late 1890s. Caroline Mikkelsen became the first woman to go to the Antarctic when she accompanied her husband, Klarius, there in 1935. But for the most part, polar exploration was limited to men. That began to change in the late 20th century. In 1986, Ann Bancroft became the first woman to walk to the North Pole. A few years later, in 1993, she led an all-women team who went to the South Pole on skis. They covered 650 miles (1,046 km) in just over two months. In 1997, six British women decided to walk to the North Pole. They were Caroline Hamilton, Zoe Hudson, Pom Oliver, Rosie Stancer, Ann Daniels, and Jan McCormac. Three years later, in 2000, they walked to the South Pole as well.

Though both the Arctic and Antarctica have been mapped and explored, there remain many areas upon which no human has walked. The journey continues . . .

there, explorers travel across the ice to the pole. Now there is less ice, and it is getting thinner, making it perhaps too dangerous to go.

Changes in the environment will also affect how scientists do research at the poles. The earth's top and bottom provide clues about what's happening all over the world—and why. And, there are still huge areas that scientists know almost nothing about. There's enough to study for years to come. Centuries ago, polar explorers laid down tracks for the next generations. The challenge for future explorers is to see where those tracks will lead.

 # Text-Dependent Questions:

1. How did the first Russian Arctic research station, NP–1, travel?

2. What is one reason that ice at the poles melts faster than in other places?

3. What was the purpose of the Antarctic Treaty of 1961?

 # Research Project

Find a scientific research project that is going on at the North or South Pole. What data are scientists collecting? How do they hope the project will help? Imagine you are part of this scientific team. What questions would you ask?

FIND OUT MORE

Websites

www.timeforkids.com/minisite/antarctica
Learn about Antarctica and the research that's happening there.

www.ducksters.com/biography/explorers/
Read the stories of all kinds of many explorers here.

www.spri.cam.ac.uk/resources/kids/
Check out this site for lots of information about both the Arctic and Antarctica.

Books

Cummings, Judy Dodge. *Exploring Polar Regions.* Minneapolis: ABDO, 2014.

Guillain, Charlotte. *Polar Regions: An Explorer Travel Guide.* Oxford, UK: Raintree, 2013.

Nardo, Don. *Polar Explorations.* Farmington Hills, MI: Lucent Books, 2011.

Snowden, Maxine. *Polar Explorers for Kids: Historic Expeditions to the Arctic and Antarctic with 21 Activities.* Chicago: Chicago Review Press, 2003.

SERIES GLOSSARY OF KEY TERMS

circumpolar: the area surrounding the North Pole, including the Arctic regions

Cold War: when nations are openly hostile toward each other while not resorting to physical warfare

continental shelf: the relatively shallow seabed surrounding a continent; the edge of a continent as it slopes down into the sea

floe: an ice sheet floating in the water

indigenous: native or original to a particular place

meteorology: the study of weather

pelts: furred animal skins

permafrost: a layer of soil that stays frozen all year long

province: an area in Canada with its own name and government, similar to a state

subsistence: a basic, minimal way of living, with only things that are necessary to survive

sustainable: something that can be maintained or practiced for a long duration without negative effects

taiga: a biome that includes the forest of mostly evergreen trees found in the southern Arctic regions

territorial waters: the parts of an ocean over which a country has control

tundra: a type of biome in very cold areas characterized by limited plant growth, frozen soil, and low rainfall

INDEX

PHOTO CREDITS

Alamy Stock Images: Trinity Mirror 30. AP Photo: 32. Cooler Antarctica: 46. Courtesy Adrian Hayes: 48. Dreamstime.com: Alberm 7, MaxMichaelman 8, Adfoto 15, Richard Lowthan 29, Ggw1962 56, Erectus 60. Minnesota Historical Society: 11. Wikimedia: 12 (by Louis Breton de Mayer), PinkFloyd88 16, Daniel Luesser 18, 20, 22, F. Nansen 25, 34, Dennis4trigger 37, Tom L-C 39, Henry Bowers 43, Gaelen Marsden 51. NASA/Courtesy Danny Galvin: 54. National Science Foundation: 52. National Library of Norway: 40. Parks Canada: 25.

ABOUT THE AUTHOR

Diane Bailey has written dozens of nonfiction books for kids and teens, on topics ranging from sports to science. She has two sons and lives in Kansas.